LITTLE ONE'S STORYTIME BOOK

ILLUSTRATED BY
PAMELA STOREY AND ERIC KINCAID

BRIMAX BOOKS · NEWMARKET · ENGLAND

To

Tristan Happy Birthday

love Ruth 1990

CONTENTS

ISBN 0 86112 293 3

Published by BRIMAX BOOKS, Newmarket, England 1985
These stories and illustrations are also published
in a collected edition 'A Book of Dreamland Stories'.
Printed in Belgium

King Ferdi And His Dragon

King Ferdi was a kind and happy man. But he hadn't been very happy for some time. He was worried—worried about his pet dragon.

Her name was Dragonia. She was a gentle dragon and full of fun until she went off her food and became droopy. She drooped all over the place and could hardly lift her tail to wag a welcome to her master.

"What's the matter, Dragonia?" he said, rubbing a little soft spot behind her ear. "Tell Ferdi! . . . Why are you so poorly?" Dragonia put her head on his knee, rolled her eyes and gave a big sigh.

The king ordered special meals to be cooked for her. They were served on golden dishes, but Dragonia gave them one sniff and turned away. She was getting thinner every day. King Ferdi was at his wit's end!

He sent for clever doctors. They were afraid to come near her.

"She won't eat you!" roared the king. But they weren't so sure and backed away. He sent for the zoo keepers, but they said: "We have no idea what is wrong, Your Majesty. You see, we don't keep dragons."

He sent for chemists to mix medicine. She shut her jaws—tight!

"What can I do!" wailed the king. "Take her for a walk," suggested the queen. "You keep her indoors too much." Ferdi looked up. "You really think so?" he asked. "Of course!" declared his wife. "Get on your horse and lead her along. It will do you both good." The king in his best hat, and Dragonia in jewelled collar, left the palace.

People poked their heads out of windows. "Fancy! There's the king with his dragon!" They called the children in. "Here comes a dragon!"

Ferdi rode on and out of town. He saw circus tents and led Dragonia towards them. "Get that thing out of here!" a man shouted. "We don't need more animals—can hardly feed what we have!" The king said he was sorry. "My pet won't eat. What do you give your animals?"

"Raw meat for the lions. Hay for horses and elephants. Fish for the seals," answered the man. "Fish!" repeated the king. "Would you sell me some fish?" The man said he could have one to try. "Then you must go," he added. "I can't risk any illness spreading from your poor creature." The king agreed—too upset to be angry. Fish was brought but Dragonia wouldn't touch it. "Could I have a handful of hay?" asked Ferdi. Hay was brought but again Dragonia refused. "Raw meat, now I suppose?" said the circus man rudely. "Yes, please!" said Ferdi politely. But it was useless.

Dragonia wouldn't touch it. The king paid the man and left. When they came to a green shady bank Ferdi stopped to rest. Dragonia flopped down. The horse went under the trees. Soon, all three were asleep.

Presently an old woman passed leading her loaded donkey. She had been to market but had sold nothing. A good smell came from the bundles; Dragonia's nose twitched even as she slept.

Suddenly, the dragon awoke, sniffing the air. Then she was up and following the smell. Hearing shuffling steps, the old woman turned.

"Why, you poor dear!" she cried. "YOU'RE STARVING!" She pulled carrots from the donkey's load and immediately the dragon took a nibble. "That's right, my dear," said the old woman, "slowly now—you'll have a pain if you gobble." Dragonia ate one carrot, then another—and another. The old woman took more from her sack and still Dragonia went on feeding. "I'd like to meet your master!" declared the old woman. "Someone rich by the look of your collar . . . I'd report him to the king!"

When Ferdi awoke he moaned aloud: "Oh dear! Where's my Dragonia?" He searched around: then looked down the road. There sat his dear dragon—gazing at a little old woman and eating! . . . EATING!! "That's enough my dear," she said. "You come along home with me, now. I'm glad I didn't sell my carrots, after all!"

"So am I, madam!" said the king from behind her. The old woman was amazed. "You should be ashamed! Didn't you know your dragon needed carrots?"

The king explained: "We never see raw carrots at the palace!" She offered him one. "Try that, Your Majesty!" Ferdi scrunched—then smiled. "Delicious! How can I reward you?" She shook her head. "I don't need reward, sir."

"Isn't there anything you'd like?" begged Ferdi. Just then his horse appeared. "Yes," she said. "I'd like to ride your beautiful horse and lead your darling dragon!" He laughed: "And so you shall!"

Helping her up he gave her Dragonia's lead. He led the donkey. They set off together and do you know—they were all eating carrots!

Sammy Scarecrow's Party

For year after year Sammy Scarecrow had stood in Farmer Green's field forgotten. His clothes had become old and tattered, and his hat was full of holes. Then one evening, the Wood Wizard stepped out of the wood and said: "Sammy, tomorrow is your twenty-first birthday, and the woodland folk have decided to give a party for you. The birds and the bees have promised to take the invitations out. The party will begin at sunset, so stay awake, Sammy."

Sammy had never been so excited. He didn't know what to do with himself all next day. At sunset the Wood Wizard stepped out of the wood again. He handed Sammy a little box. "Many happy returns of your twenty-first birthday, Sammy."

Eagerly Sammy opened the box. Inside was a tiny acorn, and underneath it was written:-

Plant me in a moonbeam's glow;
Water me to make me grow.

Before the moon rose, the guests began to arrive. The Elfin Folk flew in on the backs of moths. Leprechauns galloped in on Irish jaunting carts. They wore green suits with feathers in their hats. The Fairy Queen came in grand style in a coach drawn by a long team of ants, with ladybirds as footmen. Dwarfs rode in on the backs of moles from underground tunnels.

Kelpies arrived on tiny horses, and a party of gnomes marched in singing and playing musical instruments.

All the guests brought presents. Sammy was thrilled when he found among them a new red overcoat for the winter, a pair of baggy blue trousers, a yellow scarf, and a shiny top hat for his head. "Thank you, thank you!" he cried, "I do wish I had a feast for our guests."

"It's time you planted your acorn," the Wood Wizard said. "Look! The moon has risen."

Carefully Sammy planted the acorn in the path of a moonbeam, and watered it. In moments it became a great oak-tree.

Sammy cried out in delight. The Wood Wizard, wearing his tall pointed hat, stepped to the tree, stretched out his hand towards it, and called out in a loud voice:-

"Birthday tree, to be of use
Show the guests what you produce."

At once things began to appear on the tree, on twigs and branches and leaves—fudge, candies, liquorice, jellies of different colours, ice-creams, dewdrop drinks, cakes, cookies, tasty titbits of all kinds.

Sammy cried out delightedly: "Please help yourselves!" The guests did help themselves; but whatever they took from the tree was at once replaced by another ice-cream or cake or whatever it was. The Wood Wizard cried:-

Now feast all night and dance with glee
Round Sammy Scarecrow's birthday tree!"

Dance and feast the guests did, until at last the Wood Wizard held up his hand and cried:-

"Midnight is about to strike.
Candles, candles, come alight!"

There was a flash, and twenty-one candles lit up on the tree. Everyone cheered and clapped. Linking hands, all the guests danced round the tree, singing "Happy birthday to you, happy birthday to you, happy birthday, dear Sammy, happy birthday to you!"

They danced and sang and feasted until somewhere a clock struck twelve—midnight. The candles went out. The tree shrank into the ground. The guests whispered goodnight to Sammy and stole away. Soon all was silent.

"Thank you, Wood Wizard!" cried Sammy, "Thank you, all! I'll never, never forget this wonderful party."

Well, if ever you see a scarecrow in a field wearing a red overcoat, baggy blue trousers, a yellow scarf, and a top hat set at a jaunty angle on his head, you'll know it's Sammy Scarecrow, and *you* will remember his wonderful twenty-first birthday party, won't you?

A Running Race

It was Sunday morning. Mrs. Hedgehog was busy in her kitchen and the Hedgehog children were playing hide and seek in the garden.

"I'm just going to the field to look at my turnips," called Mr. Hedgehog who liked a walk on Sunday mornings. He was half way there when he met Mr. Hare, who was also out walking.

Mr. Hare was going to look at his cabbages.

"Good morning," said Mr. Hedgehog in his usual polite and friendly manner. "Nice morning for a walk, isn't it?"

Mr. Hare stuck his nose in the air. "What does someone with legs as short as yours know about walking?" he said scornfully.

Mr. Hedgehog didn't like other animals making fun of his short legs.

"My legs are every bit as good as yours," he said.

"Fiddle-de-dee!" scoffed Mr. Hare. "That's nonsense and you know it. Why, I can outrun you any day."

"We will put it to the test," said Mr. Hedgehog. "I will wager you a cabbage to a turnip that I can run faster than *you*."

"What a ridiculous little hedgehog you are," said Mr. Hare. "But if you will insist on making yourself look foolish why should I stop you. Shall we begin?"

"I haven't had my breakfast yet," said Mr. Hedgehog. "I can't run on an empty stomach. I'll meet you in the big field in half an hour. We will run our race along the furrows."

"Very well," said Mr. Hare and went to get some breakfast himself.

"Quick wife! Quick!" said Mr. Hedgehog when he got home. "Take off your apron and come with me."

Of course Mrs. Hedgehog, who was so like Mr. Hedgehog that they looked like two peas from the same pod, wanted to know what the fuss was about. When Mr. Hedgehog told her she said Mr. Hare was quite right, he was silly.

"No hedgehog can run faster than a hare," she said. Little did she know Mr. Hedgehog had a plan and he needed her help. They reached the far end of the field, where the race was to be

run, while Mr. Hare was still eating his breakfast.

"Hide in that furrow wife," said Mr. Hedgehog. "When you hear me call 'I am here already' bob up your head and wave."

Mrs. Hedgehog didn't understand *why* she should do such a thing, but she agreed to do it all the same. When Mr. Hare arrived Mr. Hedgehog was waiting at the opposite end of the field.

"I'm ready," said Mr. Hedgehog. "Are you?"
Mr. Hare sniffed. He would show this silly hedgehog a thing or two. "Of course I'm ready," he said.
Ready! Steady! GO!
THEY WERE OFF!
Mr. Hare lolloped along, not really bothering to hurry. The furrows were deep and he couldn't see Mr. Hedgehog but he knew he had nothing to worry about. The turnip was as good as his. His legs were made for running. Mr. Hedgehog's were not.

He couldn't believe his ears when he got to the far end of the field and heard Mr. Hedgehog call "I am here already", or his eyes, when he saw a hedgehog head pop up from the furrow next to his. How was he to know that although he had heard Mr. Hedgehog, he was seeing *Mrs*. Hedgehog? 'I'll have to run faster on the way back,' he thought.

But just before he reached the end of the furrow Mr. Hedgehog popped up at the end of his furrow. And what was more, he wasn't even panting.

"It looks as though I have won," said Mr. Hedgehog.

How was Mr. Hare to know that Mr. Hedgehog had been crouching in the furrow and hadn't run at all?

"Let us race again," said Mr. Hare, convinced there had been a mistake. A hedgehog *cannot* run faster than a hare. Everyone knows that.

Mr. Hedgehog was only too glad to oblige.

Every time Mr. Hare reached the far edge of the field, Mr. Hedgehog called out "I am here already" and Mr. Hare would see *Mrs*. Hedgehog and think he was seeing *Mr*. Hedgehog. He ran backwards and forwards for hours and didn't win once. How could he?

Mr. Hedgehog had been too clever for him, and in the end he had to part with one of his cabbages. He never did understand how it had happened. Mrs. Hedgehog said that really Mr. Hedgehog had cheated. But Mr. Hedgehog said, "Mr. Hare should not have made fun of my short legs. I wanted to teach him a lesson. Perhaps in future he will think twice before he is rude to someone."

Slibberslob The Gnome

Slibberslob lived with Esmeralda in a bird-box at the bottom of Mrs. Sherbert's garden. He was a mischievous gnome. Esmeralda was always having to get him out of some trouble into which he had fallen. When she put on her witch hat, Esmeralda could do magic, which helped.

One morning, Esmeralda climbed down the ladder of twigs that led from the bird-box to the ground. She told Slibberslob that she was going to buy some balloons for his birthday party next week.

Slibberslob waved goodbye to her from the door of the bird-box. "Don't forget to dry the dishes and put them away," called Esmeralda, "and mind you empty the washing-up water down the drain."

"I'll leave the dishes to dry themselves," said Slibberslob to himself gleefully, "and Esmeralda can put them away when she gets back. I'm not climbing all the way down to the ground either, just to get rid of the washing-up water. It's easier to throw it out."

So instead of carrying the washing-up bowl carefully down to the ground, as Esmeralda always did, the naughty gnome picked up the bowl and flung the dirty water all over the roses growing below.

One of the roses broke off under the weight of the water, but even worse, the stream of water swept all over a baby crow who was pecking insects from the roses.

"Caw, caw!" croaked the poor little crow, who was soaked with the water. He hadn't a single dry feather left on his body. Slibberslob held his sides and shook with laughter.

He thought the little wet crow looked very funny. The little baby crow flew off, croaking dismally. Slibberslob climbed down the twig-ladder and hurried over to the stone bowl in which Mrs. Sherbert put water for the birds to drink.

"I'll have a swim," he chuckled. "Hey, you birds, shoo! Hop it! Fly away! You can have a drink when I've finished my bath—if there's any water left!" He scared the birds away and was soon splashing gaily about in the bowl—but not for long.

All of a sudden he saw a black shadow over the water and next instant he found himself caught up in a big beak and carried swiftly up in the air. "Wow!" he yelled. "Hey, put me down! What's happening? Help!"

What was happening was that Mother Crow was flying with him up to her nest at the top of a very tall tree. In the nest with two other small crows was the baby crow Slibberslob had soaked with the washing-up water. All the crow babies croaked in surprise when Mother Crow dropped Slibberslob in among them.

"Has the funny little man come to play with us?" asked one of the little crows. "No. I've brought him up here to teach him not to throw water over my children," said Mother Crow. "Let me out at once!" cried Slibberslob angrily, but Mother Crow took no notice. "I shall go and peck up some lunch for you now, children," she added, shaking a claw at Slibberslob. Then she flew away.

Whatever was Slibberslob to do? He peeped over the edge of the nest but he knew he couldn't climb down from it. It was swaying in the wind too, quite dizzily. "Oh, my beard and whiskers!" he muttered. "I'm in a fix. I wish I'd emptied the water now as Esmeralda told me."

Then suddenly he saw something in the sky. It was red and round. Slowly it drifted nearer. "Why," cried Slibberslob, "it's a balloon!" Yes, it was a red balloon, with a blue basket underneath. Slibberslob guessed at once that it was one of the balloons Esmeralda had gone to buy for his birthday party. "Esmeralda has done her magic," he chuckled. "Hurray!"

As the balloon sailed by, Slibberslob climbed up on to the side of the nest and jumped into the little basket. "Ho, ho, ho, home we go!" he laughed, and soon he was sailing through the air. Slowly the balloon sank down towards Mrs. Sherbert's garden.

There, waiting for him, was Esmeralda with her witch hat on. "I might have known you'd get into mischief while I was away," she grumbled as he stepped from the basket. "I had to use magic to find you and rescue you."

"Thank you, Esmeralda. Your magic was very good. I enjoyed riding in the balloon." He peered into her shopping basket. "Now, what have you brought for lunch? I'm hungry."

"Lunch will be ready, Slibberslob," said Esmeralda, smiling sweetly, "as soon as you've put the dishes away."

"Oh, my goodness!" groaned Slibberslob. "Oh, fishes! Those dishes!"

The Little Car That Never Had A Wash

"I wish they wouldn't park you by me," said the blue Cadillac. "You're always so dirty."

A smart brown convertible nodded. "He doesn't even smell very nice," he said.

"All that dirt must reduce your speed," said a two-seater sports-car. Ricky, the little red car, felt ashamed. It wasn't his fault that none of the cars in the big garage liked him or wanted to stand near him. They were hosed down and polished regularly, but Ricky's owner, Charley Collins, was lazy and never bothered to wash the dirt from him or even clean his windows properly. The little red car had never had a wash in his life! Whenever he was put back in the garage Ricky felt unhappy, for all the other cars tried to edge away from him and made remarks about how dirty he was.

One day, Charley Collins was driving in the town when suddenly there was a loud bang. The little red car stopped. He felt all lopsided. One of his tyres had burst. "Oh, darn!" said Charley. "I expect there was a nail in the road." As there was a garage close by, Charley drove the little car, limping, into the garage and asked a mechanic to put on a new tyre.

"You need four new tyres, not one," said the mechanic, walking round Ricky. "They're all worn down to the treads."

Charley grumbled at having to buy four new tyres, but he had to agree that they were necessary.

The mechanic set to work and put on four brand-new tyres. Ricky could see himself in the garage mirror and he was thrilled. "I've got FOUR new shoes!" he told himself proudly.

"You're carrying a mighty lot of dirt around with you," remarked the mechanic. "Why not put your car through the car wash?" He pointed to a sign that said CAR WASH—ENTRY. "It'll only take you a few minutes to go through—washed, waxed and dried."

"Okay!" said Charley. "Put a car wash on the bill." Getting into the little red car, he drove him into the car wash. Then began the most exciting experience Ricky had ever had.

Great fountains of water suddenly spouted all over him. He puffed and blew, quite taken by surprise. The water sluiced all over him and down his windows. Then, almost before he could draw breath, two enormous rollers came flapping out from somewhere and began to tickle him. Ricky wriggled and squirmed and laughed. He'd never enjoyed anything so much in his life.

The rollers dried him all over thoroughly from roof to chassis, and then a waxy substance shot out and polished him until he felt smooth and sleek.

When at last he glided out of the car wash he looked like new. Charley climbed out to pay his bill, then stopped and gazed in astonishment.

"I'll be darned if that isn't worth paying for!" he cried. "I didn't know I'd got such a smart car. I'm real proud of you!"

Ricky laughed. He was proud too! Looking at himself in the garage mirror before he left, he hardly knew himself.

"This won't be your last wash," said Charley. "I'm going to take you along to that car wash every week."

When the other cars in the big garage saw Ricky, they could hardly believe their eyes. The big blue Cadillac blinked his headlamps in amazement. "Whatever's happened to you?" he demanded. "I thought for a minute you were a new car."

"You do look smart," admitted the brown convertible.

"I've been through a car wash," explained Ricky.

"You've got new tyres too," said the sports-car.

"Come and stand next to me," said the Cadillac. "I'm always washed by hand and hose myself. Do tell me what happens in a car wash. I'd love to go through. It must be quite an adventure."

Ricky sighed happily. He wasn't an outcast any more, and wouldn't be again, for from now on, Charley Collins had promised, he'd have a wash every week!

Thumbling

Once upon a time, there was a man who had a son no bigger than his thumb. He called him Thumbling and taught him how to cut and sew cloth, and how to look after himself, and not get caught by the cat or fall down a mouse-hole. Though he was so tiny, Thumbling was as brave and as bold as any other boy and just as mischievous. He had many adventures.

One day, Thumbling said to his father, "Father, I want to see something of the world."

"And so you shall my son," said Thumbling's father. He knew Thumbling would only sigh loudly and sew big uneven stitches until he had his way. The sooner he went and saw the world, the sooner he would come back home and help with the sewing.

He made Thumbling a sword from a darning needle and a knob of red wax and he made him a belt from button thread so that he could buckle the sword round his waist.

Thumbling's mother was cooking at the fireplace.

"That smells good," said Thumbling. "I'll have some of that before I go." He leant over the pot to sniff the delicious aroma of cooking lentils.

"Come back at once and say goodbye properly," grumbled his mother, as the steam from the cooking pot picked Thumbling up and wafted him up the chimney.

"Bye . . ." called Thumbling as he sailed away like a feather. "This is the only way to travel."

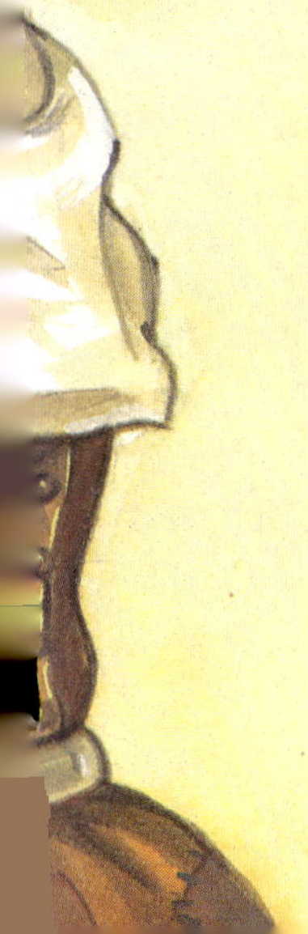

He finally sank to the ground on the far side of the valley. He found work with a man who was a tailor like his father. For a while Thumbling behaved himself, but he began to miss his mother's cooking. The tailor's wife was always forgetting to put the meat in the cooking pot and was always boiling the potatoes dry.

"One day," he said teasingly, "I shall go away if you don't feed me better and before I do, I will write on your door, 'Too many burnt potatoes and not enough meat'."

The tailor's wife was very cross. After all, she always did her best. She couldn't help it if the cooking went wrong sometimes.

"You little . . . grasshopper," she snapped and she picked up the dishcloth and tried to hit him with it.

"Ho . . ho . . can't catch me!" teased Thumbling, dodging out of the way with the greatest of ease. It is easy to dodge when you are small and easy to hide under a thimble.

"Here I am," he called to make sure she was looking his way, and when he saw she was, he poked out his tongue.

"You naughty little grasshopper . . ." she scolded as she lifted the thimble. "But I've caught you now."

"Oh no, you haven't," laughed Thumbling and he ran along the folds in the tablecloth playing hide and seek with her.

The tailor's wife caught hold of the corner of the cloth and pulled it to the floor. What a noise there was as the plates crashed and the knives clattered.

"Can't catch me!" sang Thumbling and jumped down into a crack in the table. He unbuckled his darning needle sword and every time the tailor's wife moved her hand towards him he pricked her thumb with it.

"I'll get you out of there," she scolded.

While she went to look for something to prise him out of the crack, Thumbling climbed into the table drawer.

"Yoo hoo, I'm here . . ." he called through the keyhole.

"Then I've caught you at last!" said the tailor's wife.

"Oh no, you haven't!" shouted Thumbling as she pulled the drawer open. He leapt onto her hand and flourished his darning needle sword.

"Ow!" shrieked the tailor's wife, and the drawer fell to the floor and scattered its contents far and wide. Thumbling decided the time had come for him to see some more of the world.

"Bye!" he called as he hopped, skipped and jumped along the path. "I'll leave you to clear away the mess."

"Away with you!" shouted the tailor's wife. "I would rather have a hive full of bees in my house than you." And with that she slammed the door and Thumbling went on his way.

The Tale Of The Turnip

One day, Grandpa Brown planted a turnip seed in a corner of his vegetable patch. He watered it, and pulled the weeds from around it, and it grew bigger and bigger and BIGGER.

When it was as big round, as his wife's tape measure was long, and that was very big round indeed, Grandpa Brown said, "Wife, I fancy turnip broth for my dinner today, I will pull the turnip. When it is cooked we will have a feast fit for a king." He went to the vegetable patch and took hold of the turnip's green leaves, which by now reached almost as high as his chin, and pulled. And then he pulled a bit harder. Nothing happened. The turnip was stuck tight in the ground.

"Wife!" he called. "Please come and help me."

"Why are you taking so long?" asked Grandma Brown.

"Do not waste your breath talking wife, just put your arms round my waist, and when I say pull, pull."

"Yes husband," said Grandma Brown.

"Pull!" said Grandpa Brown. Grandpa Brown AND Grandma Brown pulled and pulled. Still the turnip did not move.

"Grandson!" called Grandma Brown. "Please come and help us."

"Fancy not being strong enough to pull a turnip from the ground," said the boy trying not to laugh.

"Do not waste breath laughing," said Grandma Brown. "Put your arms round my waist and when Grandpa says pull, pull."

"Pull!" said Grandpa Brown. Grandpa Brown, Grandma Brown AND the boy pulled and pulled. Still the turnip would not move.

"Sister!" called the boy. "Please come and help us."

"I am hungry, when will the broth be ready?" asked the girl.

"Do not waste breath talking," said the boy. "Put your arms round my waist and when Grandpa says pull, pull."

"Pull!" said Grandpa Brown. Grandpa Brown, Grandma Brown, the boy AND the girl pulled and pulled. It really was a very stubborn turnip.

"Dog!" called the girl. "Please come and help us."

"Woof!" said the dog.

"Do not waste breath barking," said the girl. "When Grandpa says pull, pull."

"Pull!" said Grandpa Brown. Grandpa Brown, Grandma Brown, the boy, the girl AND the dog pulled and pulled and PULLED. But it was all wasted effort. The turnip stuck in the ground as fast as glue sticks in a gluepot.

"Cat!" called the dog. "Please come and help us."

"Miaow!" said the cat.

"Do not waste breath miaowing," said the dog. "When Grandpa says pull, pull."

"Pull!" said Grandpa Brown. Grandpa Brown, Grandma Brown, the boy, the girl, the dog AND the cat pulled as hard as they possibly could. The turnip roots pulled even harder.

It really was the stubbornest turnip any of them had ever seen.

"We might as well give up," said Grandpa Brown sadly. "We cannot pull the turnip and we will never have our turnip broth."

"What a pity," sighed Grandma Brown. "I was quite looking forward to making it."

"And I was looking forward to eating it," sighed the boy, the girl, the dog and the cat, one after the other.

"Let me help," squeaked a voice at their feet. It was a mouse who had come from his hole to see what all the sighing was about.

Grandpa Brown shook his head sadly. "The tiny amount of help you can give will make no difference at all," he said.

"At least let him try," said Grandma Brown, the boy, the girl, the dog and the cat, all at the same time.

And so once again Grandpa Brown said, "Pull!" and once again Grandpa Brown, Grandma Brown, the boy, the girl, the dog, the cat, and this time the mouse as well, pulled . . . and PULLED.

And then, so suddenly that they were all taken by surprise, the turnip came up from the ground in a shower of soil and tiny pebbles and they all fell backwards one on top of the other, with the turnip on top of them all.

When the broth was finally made, there was a special helping in a special dish for the mouse, for without his help there would have been no turnip broth at all.

The New Coat

One day, when the sun was shining, Mr. Mole popped his head out of his hole and said, "Where's this water coming from? I'm getting flooded out of my home."

"Whoo, whoo, it's the Gentle Giant," called the Owl. "He is crying so much that he has washed me off my branch."

"I was having such a lovely sleep. Whatever can be the matter with him?"

"I'll go and find out," said the Squirrel. Away he ran, up and up from one branch to another, up the tallest tree until he reached the topmost branch. The branch swayed to and fro in the breeze, so he had to cling on very tightly with his claws. He said to his friend, the Giant, "Why are you so sad? What is making you cry like this?"

"I am so cold," said the Giant, shivering and making all the trees rustle as he did so. "I haven't got a warm coat."

The Squirrel scampered down the tree and gathered all the animals around him, to tell them how unhappy and cold the Giant had become.

"We must do something before the snow comes," said Mrs. Rabbit. All was quiet as everyone tried to think of a way out of the problem.

"We could plait the long reeds that grow down by the river," suggested the Fox. "We could collect all the down from the thistles, and make it nice and warm," cried the field mice. They ran around in circles because they were so excited to be helping to make the coat.

So, using sharp thorns for needles and fine grass for the thread, they started to sew. All through the day, the animals took it in turns because it was very tiring. You see, they were so small and the coat had to be so big.

Again the Squirrel ran up the tall tree to tell his friend the Gentle Giant all about his new coat. "It won't take us very long," said the Squirrel. "Everyone is busy and working very hard."

"Oh, thank you," cried the Giant. "You are very kind. I just don't know how I can repay you."

When the coat was almost finished, the wise old Owl said, "How are you going to get the coat up to the Giant when it is ready? It looks very heavy to me. If the Giant bends down he will break all our lovely trees."

"Oh dear, oh dear," said the animals. "Whatever shall we do?"

All of a sudden, the trees were filled with birdsong. From every tree birds swooped down—big ones, small ones, plain ones and pretty ones.

"We'll do it," they sang. "We could not help to make the coat, but we can take it to him for you."

When it was ready, the birds lifted the coat high into the air and held it up for the Giant while he wrapped himself in its warm folds.

"You look after us, so we will look after you," sang the birds. The Giant was so grateful for his present that he took extra care of the little wood where so many of his friends lived.

The Moonlight Picnic

Wherever was Teddy? He had been lying by Miranda's side when she went to sleep. Now he was gone!

Miranda jumped out of bed. No, he hadn't fallen out! Then, through the window in the moonlight, she saw him. He was hurrying across the lawn towards the woods.

Miranda opened the window and called, "Teddy, come back!"

But Teddy took no notice. Miranda slipped on her dressing-gown and slippers and hurried downstairs and out through the front door. She was just in time to see Teddy disappear into the woods.

She broke into a run. The words of a song, 'The Teddy Bears' Picnic' to which she had listened on a record-player just before bedtime, flashed into her mind:

If you go down to the woods today you're sure of a big surprise;
If you go down to the woods today you'd better go in disguise.

Dare she go into the woods? They looked gloomy, but her Teddy had gone in, and he belonged to her.

"I'm going in," she said bravely, and ran on to the path.

Suddenly a huge Teddy Bear stepped out from the trees with hand raised. "Stop!" he said. "Nobody is allowed in the woods on the night of the Teddy Bears' picnic."

"So that's what it is!" said Miranda. "Well, I'm going to look after my Teddy!"

The giant bear let out a loud, angry growl as Miranda darted past him and ran into the trees. "Come back!" he shouted.

Miranda took no notice. She ran on until suddenly she came on the picnic site. She climbed up a tree and lay still on one of the branches. Below her, Teddy Bears sat in a circle, in the middle of which was a big bear with a crown on his head.

'He must be the King of the Bears,' thought Miranda.

The King of the Bears stood up, raised his hand, and said, "Welcome to Teddy Bears from everywhere! We meet only once a year. Time is short. Let us feast!"

Two Teddy Bears wearing aprons began to hand out food and drink to the other Teddy Bears. There were pots of honey, which every bear grasped at eagerly. They had no spoons; they just stuck their paws into the pots and sucked the honey from them. They ate cream cakes and all kinds of sugary titbits.

Miranda was thinking of calling out to her Teddy not to eat so many cream cakes, when there came a commotion from the woods. There was a crashing sound as a large body blundered through thick undergrowth. Then the huge bear who had stopped her burst into the circle.

"A stranger—a little girl—ran past me," he panted. "She has come to spy on us—" He broke off suddenly. Miranda was just about level with his eyes. He pointed at her. "There she is! Catch her!"

Surprised and alarmed, Miranda turned to climb down from the tree, but she missed her footing and tumbled from the branch—down . . . down . . . down.

She shut her eyes when she felt herself falling. When she opened them she found she was on the floor by her bed.

"Oh!" she cried. "I've fallen out of bed!"

She looked up. There was her Teddy Bear, lying in his usual place by her pillow.

"How silly!" she said. "I heard that record and I must have dreamed I'd gone to the Teddy Bears' picnic."

She climbed back into bed, shaking her head. "It couldn't be," she murmured, but when she fell asleep, she was still wondering. She'd noticed that Teddy had a streak of cream over his mouth. There was a smile on his face, and—yes—there were cake crumbs on his lips!

Five Merry Sailors

"I'm going for a row round the bay," said Sailor Ted one afternoon when he had nothing else to do.

"I will come with you," said Sailor Tom.

"So will I," said Tim and Terence and Tony. And they jumped into the boat, one after the other.

They each took an oar and with long, even strokes they pulled out to sea singing sea-shanties as they went. The gulls wheeled and circled round them and joined in with squawks and squeals as the sailors sang at the top of their voices . . .

"Life on the ocean waves . . . tra la . . . tra la . . ."

The five merry sailors were so busy singing and rowing and being happy, all at one and the same time, that they forgot to do something rather important. They forgot to look where they were going. They had no helmsman to tell them when to pull to the left and when to pull to the right, so they pulled neither to the left OR to the right, but pulled straight on . . . and on . . . and on. Soon there was nothing around them but dipping waves.

"Not to worry, my hearties . . . I know where we are," said Ted, when at last someone noticed they were no longer in the bay. "Pull to the right . . ."

They did. But half an hour later, they still seemed to be floating around in the middle of the same dish of sea-water.

"Just a slight mistake," said Ted, who really had no idea where they were. "I meant to say . . . pull to the left."

"Wish he'd make up his mind," muttered Tim. His arms were beginning to ache and he felt like a drink of rum.

Everyone began to give his own orders. Some pulled to the right, some pulled to the left. The boat zigzagged across the sea like a child who cannot make up his mind. Sometimes, just for a change, it went round and round in big sweeping circles.

"If we don't sight land soon, I shall become seasick," grumbled Tim.

"Land ahoy!" shouted Ted suddenly. He pointed to an island which had appeared, as though from nowhere.

"That's an island which shouldn't be there," said Terence, who knew about such things, but no one was listening.

They rowed towards the island with quick eager strokes. It didn't get any larger. It turned out to be a very small island, as islands go, and a very bare island at that. There wasn't a single blade of grass growing on it. But it was land and they would be able to stretch their stiff aching legs.

"All ashore for ten minutes," said Ted. Tim was the last over the side. "Hold that rope," said Ted. "The boat mustn't drift away."

"Just because I'm the smallest," grumbled Tim, but he took the rope because he didn't want the boat to drift away either and he sat at the edge of the water with it.

He didn't miss anything by just sitting. His four friends would have gone exploring if there had been anything to explore. But there were no holes to look inside, no rocks to look under, no sand to dig into. Just for something to do, and to show they were not feeling downhearted, they sang another sea-shanty and began to dance a hornpipe.

Tap . . . tip . . . tip . . . tap twinkled their feet all together.

"Oh . . . oh . . . what was that?" cried Terence as the island seemed to heave under their feet.

"It's an earthquake," cried Tim, as everyone tumbled over his own feet and bumped into someone else. It was nothing of the kind.

The island was . . . WAKING UP! They had landed on the back of a sleeping whale. Their dancing feet were tickling him.

The whale opened one eye and took stock of the situation. Should he dive to the bottom of the sea and sweep everyone off? No, he decided. He would go for a swim.

He turned to full speed ahead and skimmed through the sea with sailors tumbling about on his back like ninepins and with a plume of white spray spreading out in a cloud behind him. Somewhere, in the middle of the wet, white cloud was the rowing boat, because Tim was too frightened to let go of the rope.

The whale swam to within a hundred yards of the shore and then stopped swimming as suddenly as he had started.

"Into the boat, boys, while we've got the chance," ordered Ted. He was wasting his breath. Everyone was already tumbling into the boat in a very disorderly fashion not caring whose toes they trod on.

This time, they did look where they were going. A rowing boat has never moved so quickly, or in such a straight line. Only when they were safely on the quay did they turn and look back. The whale was blowing his spout and swimming out to sea.

"We had a lucky escape there, boys," said Ted.

"You can say that again," sighed Tim, Tom, Terence and Tony.

Which shows how little they understood whales, for the gentle whale had brought them home, hadn't he?

Taking A Donkey To Market

Once upon a time, there was an old man who had a donkey he wanted to sell. One fine day, when the field had been weeded, the chickens fed and the house dusted, he and his son, and the donkey of course, set off for market.

The way to market was along a winding country road. It was hot, and the old man did not feel like walking.

"We might as well make use of the donkey while we still have him," he said. He tied a knot in the four corners of his red kerchief and put it on his head to protect it from the sun and climbed onto the donkey's back. Young John took hold of the halter round the donkey's neck and they set off at a steady pace, neither hurrying nor idling, but gently jog, jog, jogging along.

The old man was gazing upwards at a soaring skylark, when he heard someone shout,

"Shame on you, old man, for riding when your son is walking."

The old man blushed and looked ashamed. He slid from the donkey's back and took the halter from his son's hand.

"You ride a while, and let me lead the donkey," he said.

They had settled down to a steady jog, jog, jog again when they met some women returning from market with laden baskets.

"Shame on you!" they cried, shaking their fists at Young John. "A young man like you riding when your old father is walking." John's face went as red as his father's had done.

"The women are right, Father," he said. "I shouldn't be riding when you are walking."

"Why don't we both ride?" said the old man.

"Now that is what I call a good idea," said Young John and taking his father's hand, he pulled him up behind him.

"What a pleasant day it is to be sure," said the old man, as they jog, jog, jogged along, listening to the skylarks and sniffing the sweet scent of hedgerow flowers. "I could jog along like this for ever."

But their peaceful ride was soon to be interrupted.

"Shame on you!" shouted some men who were making hay in a nearby field. "Shame on you!"

"Why . . . what have we done?" asked the old man in bewilderment.

"Two grown men riding on a little donkey . . . How can you be so cruel, and his head not even protected from the sun."

The old man and his son blushed as red as the scarlet poppies growing in the field. They quickly slid from the donkey's back.

"They are absolutely right," said Young John, "We shouldn't both be riding on the donkey."

"What shall we do?" asked the old man, taking the knotted kerchief from his own head and placing it between the donkey's ears. "If I ride people will say I should let you ride, if YOU ride people will say you should let me ride. If we BOTH ride that will be wrong too. What shall we do? How can we please everyone we meet?"

The donkey stood and waited. He was patient. He didn't mind waiting while they made up their minds, it gave him time to nibble at the grass.

"I know what we can do," said Young John at last. "Instead of letting the donkey carry us, WE can carry the donkey."

"Now why didn't I think of that myself," said the old man. "No one can possibly complain about that arrangement."

The donkey didn't like being carried. No self-respecting donkey would. He brayed a bit, but he didn't struggle. He thought it best not to. He had no fancy to be dropped in the middle of the road.

The old man and his son saw no one else until they reached the market place. The donkey was very heavy and they were hot and tired by the time they got there, but of one thing they were sure, no one would call shame upon them now, or accuse them of ill-treating their donkey. No one did. Instead they were greeted with great shouts of laughter.

"Fancy carrying the donkey, when the donkey should be carrying you," shouted the people in a chorus.

"By trying to please everyone," sighed the old man, "we have pleased no one. In future we will please ourselves."

Which is what they should have done in the first place!

The Balloon With A Face

Timothy was out shopping with his grandmother when he saw a man selling balloons. They were beautiful; one had a face! Timothy was delighted when Granny said, "Which one would you like, Tim?" It just had to be the one with a face.

"Hold tight," advised the man. "It's very frisky!" It certainly was. It jerked on Tim's hand all the way home.

Indoors, Timothy noticed something strange. The balloon's face wasn't smiling—it was sad. That night he tied his balloon to the bedpost. "Goodnight, Mr. Balloon!" he said. "Be happy!"

Later, Timothy awoke. His balloon was tugging at the string. He tried to tighten it but the balloon pulled harder. Before Tim could let go, he was sailing out of the window!

"Wow!" yelled Tim. "Please put me down!" He looked up at the balloon. The face was smiling. "Oh, I'm glad you're happy again—but I'm not! At least, I don't think I am. Oh, please do put me down!"

The face opened its mouth and spoke: "Can't stop, Timothy. It's just not possible. This is my chance. Thank you for undoing the string."

Tim tried to explain: "I was tying it tighter!"

The face laughed. "Never mind! You set me free, Timothy! Free! YOU mustn't start being unhappy. You're my friend and I'm taking you on a splendid adventure. So, hold tight . . . here we go!"

Down below, houses and trees looked like little blobs. A bird came up calling. "Whooo . . . are . . . youooo?" He tickled Tim's toes with his wing feathers.

"Please don't do that to my feet, it makes me giggle," said Tim.

The owl laughed, "Hooo! Hooo!" and went swooping down as they sailed up and up.

"Get ready, Tim!" said the face. "We're going to jump right over the church spire . . . One, two, three . . . Now!"

The balloon swayed as Timothy pulled up his knees. "Whee!" he cried. "That was exciting! What next? Is there anything else?"

The balloon was glad that Tim was enjoying himself. "You have no idea," he said, "what wonderful things we shall do!"

It was marvellous soaring through the dark blue sky, seeing the stars come out, more and more every minute. "We're very high, aren't we?" said Tim.

"Not really," replied the face. "We're going much higher. You'll see!"

Just then, the moon came riding out from behind a cloud. "Hallo there!" shouted the face looking up. "Shan't be long now! I'm on my way at last!" Timothy was amazed; he had to think what the face meant.

"Please," he asked, "where, exactly, are you going?"

The face gave a grin. "Why, to visit my friend The Man in the Moon, of course! He invited me ages ago. He'll be delighted to see you."

Timothy had another quiet think. "Does he like children, then?" he asked.

The balloon was humming to himself. "Hmm, hmm, hmm! . . . Hmm, tiddly hmmm! LIKE children? He loves them! He's always shining into their bedrooms, giving them a light—been doing it for years. He needs a holiday. That's why I'm going—to stand in for him. He couldn't leave the moon without a face!"

Timothy agreed that would be terrible. "How long do you think you will stay?" he wanted to know.

"Oh, for always, Tim. You want me to be happy, don't you? Well, I shall be—up there!"

At that moment, a plane appeared, travelling fast. "Hold on, Tim!" warned the face. "We may get blown about!"

Suddenly, Tim was turning over and over—he'd never managed such excellent somersaults before. "Look at me!" he shouted to the balloon. One old lady in the plane saw him, but nobody believed her! Then the plane had gone and the balloon, with Tim swinging backwards and forwards, slowly righted itself.

They stopped to rest on a star. "Well, Tim, what will your friends say about this?

. . . Oh, I forgot, you'll be with me . . . Unless you'd rather go home?" Tim nodded. The face smiled, "Then you shall! No trouble at all! . . . Goodbye, Timothy!"

Without another word he slithered off the balloon and floated away like a jelly fish.

Tim called after him, "Goodbye! You're still my friend?"

An answer came back faintly. "I shall always be your friend."

Then Tim shouted again, "Hi! You didn't tell me how to get down!"

A small voice behind him said, "Don't worry, Timothy." It was the star.

Tim gazed at her. She was shining and sparkling like a great diamond. He'd never seen anything so beautiful. "I'll help you," she said. "Put the balloon up on this sharp spike. I'll make a tiny hole: then as the balloon goes down, you will go down too." It sounded too good to be true, but it worked.

"Goodbye!" he called. "Thank you!" He waved to the star and she twinkled back; then she went paler and paler until he couldn't see her at all.

The sun was rising—a new day had begun. Tim could see fields and hedges. He was so happy he gave a jump to get home quickly. Bump! . . . He was there—in his own bed! HAD HE BEEN DREAMING IT ALL! No, for there on the floor lay the shrivelled balloon—with no face!

Timothy ran to the window. There sailed the moon, lower and paler as morning came, and there was his friend, the balloon-face smiling at him. Timothy waved and waved. The smile grew to a big grin as the face slowly winked back at Timothy.

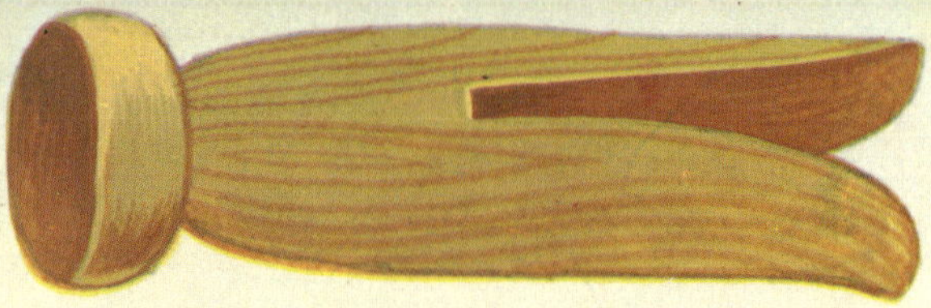

Soldiers

Ten wooden pegs,
Smooth and brown,
On the table,
Lying down.

Black for boots,
And black for hats,
Red for tunics,
Front and back.
Dark blue legs,
With stripes of white.
Spots of gold,
For buttons bright.

Ten soldiers made
From wooden pegs,
March up and down
on painted legs.

Halloween

October's days are nearly past,
Today's the day, it is the last.
At this time it is Halloween,
Ghosts and Witches often seen.
Falling leaves in chilly breeze
Lay bare the branches on the trees.
Bats flutter from their hiding places,
Lighted pumpkins show grinning faces.
The Witches ride the sky tonight
In the full moon's pale, cold light.
Broomsticks trailing misty vapour,
Halloween, Witches caper.
In and out of the clouds they go,
Moonlight shadows to and fro.
Chanting spells for the coming year,
Cackling laughter sounding clear.
An owl hoots in a night dark tree,
Chimes the church clock, 'one, two, three,'
The Witches vanish into air,
Silence follows,—nothing there!